Called to Pray

Lent and Easter with the Revised Roman Missal

*Edited by Gilles Mongeau SJ
and Brett Salkeld*

© 2012 Novalis Publishing Inc.

Cover design and layout: Audrey Wells
Cover image: iStockphoto

Published by Novalis

Publishing Office
10 Lower Spadina Avenue, Suite 400
Toronto, Ontario, Canada
M5V 2Z2

Head Office
4475 Frontenac Street
Montréal, Québec, Canada
H2H 2S2

www.novalis.ca

Library and Archives Canada Cataloguing in Publication

Called to pray : Lent and Easter with the revised
Roman missal / edited by Gilles Mongeau and Brett Salkeld.

ISBN 978-2-89646-439-5

1. Lent--Prayers and devotions. 2. Easter--Prayers and
devotions. 3. Catholic Church--Prayers and devotions.
I. Mongeau, Gilles M. (Gilles Michel-Joseph), 1964- II. Salkeld,
Brett, 1979-

BX2170.L4C35 2012   242'.34   C2011-907356-0

Printed in Canada.

All rights reserved. No part of this publication may be reproduced, stored in a retrieval system, or transmitted in any form, or by any means, electronic, mechanical, photocopying, recording, or otherwise, without the written permission of the publisher.

Excerpts from the English translation of *The Roman Missal* © 2010, ICEL.

All rights reserved.

The Scripture quotations contained herein are from the New Revised Standard Version of the Bible, copyrighted 1989 by the Division of Christian Education of the National Council of the Churches of Christ in the United States of America, and are used by permission. All rights reserved.

We acknowledge the financial support of the Government of Canada through the Canada Book Fund for business development activities.

Contents

Contributors	4
Introduction	5
Who We Are	5
Praying with *Lectio Divina*: Step by Step	6
Ash Wednesday	7
Thursday after Ash Wednesday	8
Friday after Ash Wednesday	10
Saturday after Ash Wednesday	12
First Week of Lent	14
Second Week of Lent	28
Third Week of Lent	42
Fourth Week of Lent	56
Fifth Week of Lent	70
Palm Sunday of the Lord's Passion	84
Easter Triduum	92
Mass of the Lord's Supper (Holy Thursday)	92
Celebration of the Lord's Passion (Good Friday)	93
The Resurrection of the Lord (Easter Vigil)	94
The Resurrection of the Lord (Easter Sunday)	95

Contributors

Student members of Alpha Sigma Nu:

Kelly Bourke
Ernest Holland
Wayne Lott
Mary Jo McDonald
Peter Nguyen, S.J.
Brett Salkeld, co-editor

Alumni/ae members:

Hugh Crosthwait
Joan Gallagher-Main
Lecia Kiska
Robin Koning, S.J.
Linda Labelle
Greta deLonghi
Erin MacCarthy
Gilles Mongeau, S.J., co-editor
Gemma Neal
Erik Oland, S.J.
Kathy Perry
Deacon Tony Pignataro
Ann Sirek

Honorary members:

Gill Goulding, CJ
Gordon Rixon, S.J.
Joseph Schner, S.J.

Introduction

Welcome to *Called to Pray: Lent and Easter with the Revised Roman Missal*. Like the Advent and Christmas edition, this book proposes short reflections on the collects (opening prayers) of the mass for each day of this liturgical season, in light of the gospel readings of that day. Our hope is that these reflections will enhance your experience of the central prayer of the Christian community, the liturgy, especially in this exciting and challenging time of transition to the revised Roman Missal. We hope to help you develop the spiritual affinity with the collects that can lead to full, conscious and active participation; this is why you will find, on the next page, a method for *lectio divina* prayer that you can use with all the texts of the liturgy, not just the opening prayer.

Who we are

The authors of the reflections in this book are members of Alpha Sigma Nu, a Jesuit academic honour society at Regis College, the pontifical faculty of theology run by the Society of Jesus at the University of Toronto. The membership of Alpha Sigma Nu consists of faculty, students and former students of Regis College, as well as honorary members from the broader community, all of whom are recognized for their commitment to the Ignatian ideal of learned ministry that seeks God in all things. These members come from all walks of life. Some of the professions represented in the ranks of the Regis chapter are nurses, police officers, and lay pastoral workers, as well as students and professors. Further, these members include married and single lay persons, those in religious life, deacons, and priests.

Praying with *Lectio Divina*: Step by Step

1. Find a quiet place and time to pray: early morning at the kitchen table before everyone else is up, or your favourite armchair after everyone has left the house or gone to bed, or your office once you've been able to close the door for a few minutes.
2. Settle in and take the time to acknowledge that God is here with you. Offer yourself to God for this time of prayer in these or similar words: "Father, take all of my knowing and loving, and order it now to your greater service and praise." Repeat this short phrase slowly until you sense you mean it with your heart and desire it in your gut.
3. Read the prayer of the day slowly, letting the words and phrases sink in. Read it through a second or even a third time, so that the words come alive in your memory and imagination.
4. Pause and ask yourself: What words, phrases, or images from this prayer move me? Which ones catch my attention?
5. Let your memory and imagination savour these words: Do any special memories from your life come up as you let these words live in you? Do any desires arise, or a sense of gratitude to God? Simply stay with these movements.
6. At this point, pick up the gospel of the day and read it in light of these words and phrases. Then turn to the short reflection we have provided to orient your encounter with the prayer and the gospel.
7. As you let these interior movements unfold in your heart and mind, you may find that you want to say something to God or to Jesus. Take the time to share with them what is on your heart and mind.
8. Close by praying the Our Father.

Ash Wednesday

Collect

> Grant, O Lord, that we may begin with holy fasting
> this campaign of Christian service,
> so that, as we take up battle against spiritual evils,
> we may be armed with weapons of self-restraint.
> Through our Lord Jesus Christ, your Son,
> who lives and reigns with you in the unity of the Holy Spirit,
> one God, for ever and ever. Amen.

Matthew 6:1-6, 16-18

It can be a battle to bring the healing presence of Christ into a wounded world. We can easily slip into dismissing or cutting down others. It takes self-restraint to wage Christian service. Holy fasting is a spiritual practice that arms us with self-restraint – but not by making us invulnerable. Rather, fasting engenders a certain kind of vulnerability. As soon as we resolve to fast, we are bombarded by temptation and pride, uncovering a place of deeper weakness where only God can work to bring about new life.

Jesus, in the gospel, challenges us to an even more profound level of self-restraint, not for its own sake, but for a deeper, more intimate relationship with God: we share something with God alone. It is like sharing something very special with a spouse, lover or friend, as a sign of trust and fidelity. Only in this way are we truly armed for spiritual battle.

Greta DeLonghi

Thursday after Ash Wednesday

Collect

Prompt our actions with your inspiration, we pray, O Lord,
and further them with your constant help,
that all we do may always begin from you
and by you be brought to completion.
Through our Lord Jesus Christ, your Son,
who lives and reigns with you in the unity of the Holy Spirit,
one God, for ever and ever. Amen.

Luke 9:22-25

A mother nursing her newborn every two hours for weeks on end denies herself, and her child thrives. The man who leaves for weeks each month for work denies himself so that his family can have a better life. Those who spend their days at nursing homes caring for their loved ones deny themselves in order to be present to family and friends. Sleepless nights, homesickness, loneliness, and grief are the crosses that so many of us carry today for the greater good.

It is through these very crosses that we can experience a deeper relationship with our God. Jesus Christ denied his very self and carried his cross to his death and Resurrection. We are inspired to be other-centred, to look at the greater good when we deny ourselves. Even though denying ourselves can be painful, Jesus shows us the way by his inspiration and furthers our actions with his constant help. He prompts us to follow him and to take on whatever life throws at us, to unite our giving with his giving, "that all we do may begin in him and by him be brought to completion" – for the greater glory of God.

Linda Labelle

Friday after Ash Wednesday

Collect

Show gracious favour, O Lord, we pray,
to the works of penance we have begun,
that we may have strength to accomplish with sincerity
the bodily observances we undertake.
Through our Lord Jesus Christ, your Son,
who lives and reigns with you in the unity of the Holy Spirit,
one God, for ever and ever. Amen.

Matthew 9:14-15

Undertaking bodily observances.... Fasting invites us to experience our hungers. What hungers and cravings do we hold back, tucked away in the deepest recesses of our consciousness? What hidden, soul-destructive behaviours haunt us? Become still now and bring your focus to those interior recesses. Take note of your breath; notice any tension that seems to catch the breath. Very gently, allow yourself to groan from somewhere deep inside. Now, louder. Now lift up your voice like a trumpet and cry out with the pain of your hidden hungers: perfectionism, righteousness, shame, arrogance, quarrels, violence... Bow your head. Take a deep inbreath. With the outbreath, gently release the pain. Notice how your neck lengthens slightly with the outbreath; rock your head gently as you breathe. Now prostrate yourself. Feel the prayer rug rough against your skin. Take the next breath; allow it to pass out beyond the boundary of your skin. Let your breath reach out and touch someone who is oppressed... and on the next breath one who is destitute... Imagine Divine Mercy touching each of us intimately, like a breath. And now the dawn breaks forth, bathing us all in light. Cry out with desire. Listen... Here I am!

Ann Sirek

Saturday after Ash Wednesday

Collect

Almighty ever-living God,
look with compassion on our weakness
and ensure us your protection
by stretching forth the right hand of your majesty.
Through our Lord Jesus Christ, your Son,
who lives and reigns with you in the unity of the Holy Spirit,
one God, for ever and ever. Amen.

Luke 5:27-32

God's justice is a "majestic compassion" that restores sinners to right relation. Every word found in the Scripture today has a common, plain sense. Yet, familiar words combine to shape an unexpected meaning that challenges our expectation of social privilege and advancement for those who contribute most productively in society. We are reminded that our lives focus not on personal advancement but on a goal that goes beyond ourselves, an end that we do not control, a purpose shared with all peoples, all creation. By being restored in right relation, we let go of lesser, perhaps even distorted objectives and recommit ourselves in God's purpose. Honouring the Sabbath, delighting in the recognition of those put to the side of society, and caring for those who are diminished in physical, social, or spiritual vigour bring a new light to illumine our way, a light that guides us through common events and familiar meanings to rediscover the divine.

Gordon Rixon, S.J.

First Sunday of Lent

Collect

Grant, almighty God,
through the yearly observances of holy Lent,
that we may grow in understanding
of the riches hidden in Christ
and by worthy conduct pursue their effects.
Through our Lord Jesus Christ, your Son,
who lives and reigns with you in the unity of the Holy Spirit,
one God, for ever and ever. Amen.

Mark 1:12-15

Could any forty days be more stark? Driven out…in the wilderness…tempted…wild beasts. This is the austerity of Lent. During these sacred forty days in the wilderness of aloneness I am confronted by myself – who I truly am. Satan is there, alluring with bright possibilities and promises. The world around hastens to charm and seduce. But angels minister, encouraging, strengthening. In the midst of this time of desert, the haunting question comes: Who am I?

Lord, help me to understand that you invite me into the wilderness to share yourself, to share your call. Who am I? I confess my sinfulness. Who am I? I believe the good news. Who are we? Sinners. Who are we? Believers. Sent.

Could mission be more urgent? In Galilee, proclaiming the good news. God's reign is near. During these forty days, I pray, Lord, that in the desert I may come to know your compassionate love. During these forty days, may I experience true riches and proclaim them to the world.

Joseph Schner, S.J.

Monday in the First Week of Lent

Collect

Convert us, O God our Saviour,
and instruct our minds by heavenly teaching,
that we may benefit from the works of Lent.
Through our Lord Jesus Christ, your Son,
who lives and reigns with you in the unity of the Holy Spirit,
one God, for ever and ever. Amen.

Matthew 25:31-46

Instruct our minds by heavenly teaching.... Lent is an intense period of personal reflection that can lead us to get to know God and ourselves better. Today we are reminded that the journey ultimately leads us into deeper relationship with those around us. Contemplation and action are intimately linked. Those at Jesus' right hand are blessed by God, the proof of which lies in how they in turn are blessings to others, especially to the most vulnerable and marginalized. Those who are accursed are apathetic – they are not moved to reach out to those in need and remain focused on themselves.

This difference is reinforced with the imagery of communal, flocking sheep versus the more independent goat. It is not possible to be in relationship with God and ignore the people around us. Everyone is made in God's image and likeness, something Jesus emphasizes by identifying himself most closely with those who are easy to ignore or who make us uncomfortable. If I cut myself off from others and fail to respond to their call, I cut myself off from God – from love.

Lecia Kiska

Tuesday in the First Week of Lent

Collect

Look upon your family, Lord,
that, through the chastening effects of bodily discipline,
our minds may be radiant in your presence
with the strength of our yearning for you.
Through our Lord Jesus Christ, your Son,
who lives and reigns with you in the unity of the Holy Spirit,
one God, for ever and ever. Amen.

Matthew 6:7-15

We have all invested time, energy, and finances into things that we hope will bring some degree of satisfaction in return. Often enough we have also experienced how these personal investments have ended up in disappointment. There are certainly enough enticements within our surrounding culture that promise everything one can seemingly ask for, but prove to bring very little lasting value in the end.

Will the chastening effects of bodily discipline be satisfying? In Isaiah 55, God speaks to his people and invites them to turn from that which does not satisfy, and to turn instead back to him. What assurances are the people given that they can find their true satisfaction in God? God's very word! God's word goes out, and it will never return to him empty. God's word always accomplished what he purposes. God keeps his promises.

Through his word, God spoke this world into being. In the person of Jesus, God's Word became flesh and dwelt among us. Now, in this season of Lent, God's word speaks to us and calls us to turn to the one who is the source of life, meaning, and value. Let us turn to the one who knows what we need before we even ask him. God's word will accomplish what he purposes.

Wayne Lott

Wednesday in the First Week of Lent

Collect

Look kindly, Lord, we pray,
on the devotion of your people,
that those who by self-denial are restrained in body
may by the fruit of good works be renewed in mind.
Through our Lord Jesus Christ, your Son,
who lives and reigns with you in the unity of the Holy Spirit,
one God, for ever and ever. Amen.

Luke 11:29-32

Among the people whom Jesus chastises for asking for a sign, there were surely some who had already seen him perform miracles. In place of belief, though, their hearts were filled with a desire for more of these supernatural but earthly wonders. On our own spiritual journeys we can have those moments that are akin to Jesus' miracles, when the veil is lifted and the spiritual world can be felt almost tangibly. In these moments, we *know* that God is present, and it is a different type of knowledge than we usually have of him. These experiences form part of our stories, but their impact can fade with time or even become commonplace. Our task, however, does not change despite what we may or may not feel. The big miracles and events must eventually give way to quiet and patient devotion to God's will; the shock of a miraculous healing or an impassioned conversion cede their place to meditation on the sign of Jonah. We restrain our bodies, forsaking even the pleasure of "spiritual highs." Through this, another form of experience occurs, one that fulfills our prayer for today and truly renews our mind through diligently striving after Christ.

Ernest Holland

Thursday in the First Week of Lent

Collect

Bestow on us, we pray, O Lord,
a spirit of always pondering on what is right
and of hastening to carry it out,
and, since without you we cannot exist,
may we be enabled to live according to your will.
Through our Lord Jesus Christ, your Son,
who lives and reigns with you in the unity of the Holy Spirit,
one God, for ever and ever. Amen.

Matthew 7:7-12

Contemplation and action are two concepts close to the heart of Ignatian spirituality. The early Jesuit Jerome Nadal coined the term "contemplative in action," a phrase by which Jesuits often identify themselves. In the verbs "to ponder" and "to hasten," found in the collect, we touch upon a basic attitude of prayer leading to action that is so central to the Christian life. Pondering and contemplating, and hastening to act must be held in a certain tension or balance as we reflect upon and live out the gospel message. Treated exclusively, they can lead to either spiritual self-centredness (prayer without action) or worldly self-sufficiency (action without prayer). Jesus' dictum "in everything do to others as you would have them do to you" expresses an articulation of contemplation in action. This golden rule is both an invitation to deep self-knowledge and a call to be other-centred in the active life. It is a great equalizer for those who find themselves preaching from on high or getting lost in a litany of "shoulds" without having the humility to truly ponder God's will in any given situation.

Erik Oland, S.J.

Friday in the First Week of Lent

Collect

Grant that your faithful, O Lord, we pray,
may be so conformed to the paschal observances,
that the bodily discipline now solemnly begun
may bear fruit in the souls of all.
Through our Lord Jesus Christ, your Son,
who lives and reigns with you in the unity of the Holy Spirit,
one God, for ever and ever. Amen.

Matthew 5:20-26

This is the season of return to righteousness. We practise turning our whole selves to the commandments of right relationship. Jesus teaches us the essence of righteousness: reconciliation. Love is the commandment; by asking and offering forgiveness, we authentically embody love. We must ask forgiveness for the daily "murders" we commit. This challenges us to honesty and humility. How easy it is to nurse outrage and resentment. To let go of our inhibitions and say that sarcastic comment, raise our voice just enough, cut someone down with two words.

We are well practised in control and hurtfulness. How natural it seems, when accused of wrongdoing, to hug our good deeds and reputation to ourselves, protest our innocence, and deny our sin. Instead, Jesus expects us to conform to his paschal example and give up such defences, turning to reconcile with those we are injuring, "and so bear fruit in the souls of all." He teaches us another essential aspect of righteousness: the turning itself. We must adopt a continual, conscious reorientation of attitude and action so that we are giving life, not destroying it. Every moment offers new opportunity to get it right. And so we practise turning.

Joan Gallagher-Main

Saturday in the First Week of Lent

Collect

Turn our hearts to you, eternal Father,
and grant that, seeking always the one thing necessary
and carrying out works of charity,
we may be dedicated to your worship.
Through our Lord Jesus Christ, your Son,
who lives and reigns with you in the unity of the Holy Spirit,
one God, for ever and ever. Amen.

Matthew 5:43-48

A key Lenten theme is indicated at the start of today's collect – that of repentance, of turning towards God. "Turn our hearts to you, eternal Father." This turning towards God is the first step in that dedication to the worship of God for which we pray at the end of the collect – that praise, reverence, and service of God for which we were created and which is to be our eternal bliss.

Between these bookends, we ask for the grace to follow the path towards this end. First, "seeking always the one thing necessary" – reminding us of Martha, distracted in her service rather than remaining centred on God present in her midst. Second, "carrying out works of charity" – these, too, are an essential element of true dedication to the worship of God. Loving God and loving our neighbour. It is only by this "turning towards" our eternal Father that we are able to be transformed into his image, able to become true children of the Father, able to become perfect like him, as the gospel calls us to be. Even to attain that highest perfection of charity, perhaps our highest form of worship of God – love of our enemies.

Robin Koning, S.J.

Second Sunday of Lent

Collect

O God, who have commanded us
to listen to your beloved Son,
be pleased, we pray,
to nourish us inwardly by your word,
that, with spiritual sight made pure,
we may rejoice to behold your glory.
Through our Lord Jesus Christ, your Son,
who lives and reigns with you in the unity of the Holy Spirit,
one God, for ever and ever. Amen.

Mark 9:2-10

As we gather today, we pray to be nourished inwardly by God's word. We dispose ourselves in an attitude of trust, which is the inner movement of grace for which we pray. We direct our attention to *listening* to the word of God, which was God's command to Peter, James, John, and all of Jesus' followers in today's gospel. In our busy, noisy lives, it is often difficult to know what to listen to and what to block out.

We need to pay attention to what is happening within us as we listen. The inner disposition of the disciples as they witness the amazing transfiguration of Jesus on the mountain is fear. They are terrified, but that is not the end of the story. In this moment, when they are afraid, God commands them to listen to "the Beloved." At once, God commands and reassures the disciples so that their fear can give way to trust in Jesus and belief concerning what he has to say to them. It is our inner disposition of trust that encounters the reality of God's glory, and we give thanks because we, too, are "beloved" and are therefore empowered to do what God commands.

Kathy Perry

Monday in the Second Week of Lent

Collect

O God, who have taught us
to chasten our bodies
for the healing of our souls,
enable us, we pray,
to abstain from all sins,
and strengthen our hearts
to carry out your loving commands.
Through our Lord Jesus Christ, your Son,
who lives and reigns with you in the unity of the Holy Spirit,
one God, for ever and ever. Amen.

Luke 6:36-38

Strengthen our hearts to carry out your loving commands. I wait, and in the desert-silence of my waiting I am tested and prepared. I wait, and through the long days and restless nights I am instructed, taught to let fall from myself all self-promoting interests. I wait, and my hunger grows so that what I am offered I have longed for, what I am given has been desired. I wait, and in the desert-crossing of my waiting I leave behind my limited world and emerge a new person, made ready and equal to the task.

I wish to be rid of all thoughts, but what disappear are all other thoughts save this one: to love you, my Lord. I wish to quiet all dreams, but what dies is all other dreams but one, to serve you in my brothers and sisters. And I am tempted to be afraid, to fear such loving, such hoping, such dreaming lest it be denied. And I am tempted to be cautious, to not risk my love, my hope, my joy, lest it be disappointed. But I will not be afraid; I will not be afraid of loving, of hoping. For I trust in the God of love, and believe in the God of hope.

Deacon Tony Pignataro

Tuesday in the Second Week of Lent

Collect

Guard your Church, we pray, O Lord,
    in your unceasing mercy,
and, since without you mortal humanity is sure to fall,
may we be kept by your constant helps from all harm
and directed to all that brings salvation.
Through our Lord Jesus Christ, your Son,
who lives and reigns with you in the unity of the Holy Spirit,
one God, for ever and ever. Amen.

Matthew 23:1-12

The opening prayer asks God to send upon the Church his very mercy. Why does the Church need divine mercy? There are two reasons. First, we are a frail people, who consistently make mistakes and fall. We do not attain holiness on our achievements, but rather we attain holiness through the reception of the Spirit of Christ. This Spirit forgives, heals, and conforms us to stand with the Son in the love of the Father. To be Church is not, in the first place, to strive for rightness or goodness, but to experience the merciful love of the Trinity. Second, as a people who receive, encounter, and experience this mercy, we can only say thank you to God by sharing this very mercy with others. Since God was able to meet us at our place of shame and darkness and make us one with him, we become that instrument of salvation to others. We go out to meet and share with others the grace of divine transformative mercy. Our job is not ultimately to tell people how wrong they are and how right we are, but to witness to them an Otherness that can overcome and transform their own darkness and shame.

Peter Nguyen, S.J.

Wednesday in the Second Week of Lent

Collect

Keep your family, O Lord,
schooled always in good works,
and so comfort them with your protection here
as to lead them graciously to gifts on high.
Through our Lord Jesus Christ, your Son,
who lives and reigns with you in the unity of the Holy Spirit,
one God, for ever and ever. Amen.

Matthew 20:17-28

How much we need to be "schooled" by the Lord! How easy we find it to miss the important point because we are like children fascinated by some colourful enticement and stray from what we know to be right and good. We so often find ourselves on a trajectory to what is harmful to ourselves or others. In the gospel today, Jesus is trying to prepare the disciples for the trauma of his coming passion, and it is almost as though they, like children, are not listening. Instead they are caught up with status and power and who sits where in the kingdom of God, and the mother of James and John, in her maternal pride, does not help matters. But Jesus "schools" the disciples in his way by underlining "whoever wishes to be first among you must be your slave." He upsets the balance of power argument by emphasizing that in the kingdom, it is the humble, loving servant who is most important. Jesus himself is to exemplify this way as he lives out his own passion. He calls us each day to that same loving service. How well have we learned this lesson?

Gill Goulding, CJ

Thursday in the Second Week of Lent

Collect

> O God, who delight in innocence and restore it,
> direct the hearts of your servants to yourself,
> that, caught up in the fire of your Spirit,
> we may be found steadfast in faith
> and effective in works.
> Through our Lord Jesus Christ, your Son,
> who lives and reigns with you in the unity of the Holy Spirit,
> one God, for ever and ever. Amen.

Luke 16:19-31

In life, all was under control for the man in today's gospel. He was rich and well dressed; he feasted daily. In death he is in dire straits and calls out for help. To cool himself he asks for water. To comfort his own soul he asks that a message be given to his still-living brothers. Aware of his needs, he becomes terrifyingly aware that they will not be met. He has lost control.

Was control lost as he moved from life to death, or long before his appointed day? What had come to blind him to the pain of those like Lazarus on his very doorstep? Over a lifetime of choices he had become self-absorbed, self-satisfied, and unaware of the needs around him. The innocence of childhood and the wonder of life had long ago departed. He awakes to reality when it is too late.

We direct our hearts to God, as God's servants, asking ourselves:

In the tragedy of this story, can we find hope? In the insensitivity and self-centredness of our lives, are we able to trust that God will restore us to innocence and melt away the many barriers separating us from self and from others?

Where is God whispering to us to allow, in grace and in love, the Spirit to influence and transform us?

Hugh Crosthwait

Friday in the Second Week of Lent

Collect

Grant, we pray, almighty God,
that, purifying us by the sacred practice of penance,
you may lead us in sincerity of heart
to attain the holy things to come.
Through our Lord Jesus Christ, your Son,
who lives and reigns with you in the unity of the Holy Spirit,
one God, for ever and ever. Amen.

Matthew 21:33-43, 45-46

Jesus' parable draws the chief priests and the Pharisees into a story that turns out to be about them. How shocking that must have been for them! By identifying the injustice in the story, they have implicated themselves. Jesus was very aware that the leaders were more focused on the people following their interpretations of the Law than in following the real meaning of the Law. Perhaps this gave them a sense of control and power during a time of great uncertainty, a time much like our own.

We know what it is like. So often the need for security prompts us to hang on to those second-skin-like, familiar ways of thinking and feeling. But are they true? Or are they just familiar? Jesus challenged the leaders to examine their own interpretation of scripture. They had missed the truth; they had failed "to attain the holy things to come," the real meaning of the Scripture – they had missed recognizing him. To search for the real meaning is not comfortable. It means allowing ourselves to anguish for a while as old understandings give way to new, corrected, or developed ones. Let us pray for sincerity of heart, the willingness to discover the truth about ourselves and our worldview: a truth to which we are all called by Christ.

Mary-Jo McDonald

Saturday in the Second Week of Lent

Collect

O God, who grant us
    by glorious healing remedies while still on earth
to be partakers of the things of heaven,
guide us, we pray, through this present life
and bring us to that light in which you dwell.
Through our Lord Jesus Christ, your Son,
who lives and reigns with you in the unity of the Holy Spirit,
one God, for ever and ever. Amen.

Luke 15:1-3, 11-32

The younger son wants to partake of his Father's riches, but he seeks, at first, to receive them on his own terms. It is only when he has been healed of his pride, when the humiliations of the pigsty have – by God's grace – opened up a space in his heart for genuine knowledge of his self-deception, that he can receive these riches as gifts from his father's generous love.

Lent offers us "glorious healing remedies" – fasting, the sacrament of reconciliation, renewed practices of prayer and contemplation – that free us from our distorted reliance on creatures, on the good opinion of others, and on our own deceptive self-will, so that even in this life we may be partakers of the things of heaven, following Christ to that light in which God dwells.

Gilles Mongeau, S.J.

Third Sunday of Lent

Collect

O God, author of every mercy and of all goodness,
who in fasting, prayer and almsgiving
have shown us a remedy for sin,
look graciously on this confession of our lowliness,
that we, who are bowed down by our conscience,
may always be lifted up by your mercy.
Through our Lord Jesus Christ, your Son,
who lives and reigns with you in the unity of the Holy Spirit,
one God, for ever and ever. Amen.

John 2:13-25

When St. John tells us that "Jesus was speaking of the temple of his body," we rightly recognize a premonition of the Resurrection. But do we recognize the spiritual law inherent in that premonition? Do we, "bowed down by our conscience," recognize in those words the promise of our own being "lifted up by his mercy"?

Forty-six years of human labour and the temple was not only unfinished, but corrupt. Imagine the human cost of a construction project of this magnitude in the ancient world! And now think about how, instead of being used for the glory of God, it was being used by unscrupulous money changers to perpetuate the burden on the poor, on whose backs the temple was necessarily built. Those who came to "confess their lowliness" were being swindled even as they sought reparation with their God.

But Jesus, who knows what lies within the human person, not only promises the destruction of such a system, but offers, in its place, a share in his body – the new temple that cannot be destroyed. The Resurrection of that body is the promise of the Resurrection for those made members of it. Those crushed by guilt and those crushed by the guilty, perpetrators and victims (and which of us is not both!), can be lifted above the cycle of violence and oppression. But only if they are foolish enough to forsake human wisdom and become members of the One whose weakness was stronger than human strength.

Brett Salkeld

Monday in the Third Week of Lent

Collect

> May your unfailing compassion, O Lord,
> cleanse and protect your Church,
> and, since without you she cannot stand secure,
> may she be always governed by your grace.
> Through our Lord Jesus Christ, your Son,
> who lives and reigns with you in the unity of the Holy Spirit,
> one God, for ever and ever. Amen.

Luke 4:24-30

Sometimes we can get attached to the way things are, or how we want them to be, and we can miss what God is offering to us. Often, I find myself so caught up in the expectation of what should be or should come that I forget to leave room for what *could* come if I was more open to the possibilities God is creating for me, in me, and through me. I try to stand secure in what I have, and what I have come to expect from my life. How much do I miss because I am distracted by my own agenda? I am grateful for the little moments in life when I have been surprised by God's grace and see the wonderful opportunity in what really is, not what I had planned. These moments remind me to be open. It is my prayer to notice the unexpected, to be open to God's grace and all the possibilities that may unfold. Are you open to God in unexpected ways?

Kelly Bourke

Tuesday in the Third Week of Lent

Collect

> May your grace not forsake us, O Lord, we pray,
> but make us dedicated to your holy service
> and at all times obtain for us your help.
> Through our Lord Jesus Christ, your Son,
> who lives and reigns with you in the unity of the Holy Spirit,
> one God, for ever and ever. Amen.

Matthew 18:21-35

Dearest Lord in Heaven, I love you but have sinned against you. *May your grace not forsake me....* Please forgive me and grant me peace in my mind, my heart, and my soul. As you have shown me mercy, please let me forgive those who have sinned against me. *Dedicate me to your holy service....* It is not enough for me to forgive with my head. I need to have the strength and humility to forgive my neighbour from deep within my heart, and treat them with the same kindness and compassion that I long for from you and others, Lord. *May your grace obtain for us your help....* I can't do this on my own, so please grant me the grace to be merciful towards all those who have hurt me. Let me show love and respect to everyone I encounter, even those who have wronged me.

Erin MacCarthy

Wednesday in the Third Week of Lent

Collect

Grant, we pray, O Lord,
that, schooled through Lenten observance
and nourished by your word,
through holy restraint
we may be devoted to you with all our heart
and be ever united in prayer.
Through our Lord Jesus Christ, your Son,
who lives and reigns with you in the unity of the Holy Spirit,
one God, for ever and ever. Amen.

Matthew 5:17-19

Keenly aware, on account of Paul's letters, that we are not justified by the law, and that our attempts at such justification are self-defeating, we can forget that the Jewish people understood the law as a great gift. This is made clear in today's first reading from Deuteronomy: "And what other great nation has statutes and ordinances as just as this entire law that I am setting before you today?"

In the gospel we hear Jesus' warning, "Do not think that I have come to abolish the law or the prophets; I have come not to abolish but to fulfill." The solution to our inability to fulfill the law is not God's resignation, but God's action! To lower the standards because we could not meet them would be nothing more than to leave us to wallow in our own filth. We are justified in Christ, not in abstraction from the Law, but because he fulfilled it.

In our Lenten observance, then, we Christians can rely on one of the aspects of law that, as Jesus says, will not pass. The law is a teacher. Through it we are schooled in discipline ("holy restraint") and devotion as well as reminded of our inadequacy and our need for God's salvation.

Brett Salkeld

Thursday in the Third Week of Lent

Collect

> We implore your majesty most humbly, O Lord,
> that, as the feast of our salvation draws ever closer,
> so we may press forward all the more eagerly
> towards the worthy celebration of the Paschal Mystery.
> Through our Lord Jesus Christ, your Son,
> who lives and reigns with you in the unity of the Holy Spirit,
> one God, for ever and ever. Amen.

Luke 11:14-23

An evocative sculpture at the Loyola House retreat centre in Guelph, Ontario, has St. Ignatius Loyola walking, his body angled into the wind, his cloak billowing out behind him – pressing forward. We press forward now as the feast of our salvation draws near. However eagerly we might approach this encounter, we may still feel as if we are walking into the wind – certainly into resistance of some kind. Like those demons of our culture, for instance, that would mute our amazement at the evidence of the finger of God, the presence of the kingdom, in all things. Demons such as cynicism, skepticism, busy-ness, and even faulty logic, as Jesus so nimbly uncovers in the gospel.

When Jesus says, "Whoever is not with me is against me, and whoever does not gather scatters," he invites us to walk with him, however windy it might be, however scattered we might feel. Jesus, the Good Shepherd who gathers the lambs in his arms, offers us that healing, reconciling embrace. We experience being gathered in receiving the sacraments and in merciful movements towards social and ecological justice, but also in ordinary, everyday moments: maybe a sincere apology – received or given, a foot rub, the bright sun on a chilly day, a good meal, kind words, compassionate health care, laughter with a friend. Small steps as we press forward.

Greta DeLonghi

Friday in the Third Week of Lent

Collect

> Pour your grace into our hearts, we pray, O Lord,
> that we may be constantly drawn away from unruly desires
> and obey by your own gift the heavenly teaching you give us.
> Through our Lord Jesus Christ, your Son,
> who lives and reigns with you in the unity of the Holy Spirit,
> one God, for ever and ever. Amen.

Mark 12:28-34

ear, O Israel: The Lord our God, the Lord is one. Love the Lord your God with all your heart, and with all your soul, and with all your mind, and with all your strength … love your neighbour as yourself… (Deut. 6:4-9).

Jesus knew this passage from his earliest childhood. Written on parchment, it is put in a small container called a mezuzah and is nailed to doorframes and gates of Jewish homes. Also used today, it serves as a reminder of God's heavenly teaching and Presence whenever a person passes through the door.

Obedience to this love command is essential for all God's people. Jesus tells us that this knowing brings us closer to the kingdom of God. The more aware we are of God in our midst, the more aware we are of the call to love God and one another. During this season of Lent, we are invited to reflect on our lives. How well do I love God, neighbour, and world?

Pour your grace into our hearts… We pray to become acutely aware of God's Presence. Knowing and living this, "we will be drawn away from unruly desire"; there will be no place for gossip, negativity, criticism, or violent language. Our communities will reflect the words of Jesus: *"See how they love one another.…"*

Linda Labelle

Saturday in the Third Week of Lent

Collect

Rejoicing in this annual celebration
of our Lenten observance,
we pray, O Lord,
that, with our hearts set on the paschal mysteries,
we may be gladdened by their full effects.
Through our Lord Jesus Christ, your Son,
who lives and reigns with you in the unity of the Holy Spirit,
one God, for ever and ever. Amen.

Luke 18:9-14

A contemplation in the tradition of St. Ignatius Loyola, to "set our hearts on the paschal mysteries," as we "rejoice in this annual celebration of our Lenten observances":

I stand before an ancient altar, a purple curtain, behind which dwells Eternity, Infinity, Mystery. People swarm about – men, women, children, embracing, laughing, shrieking, goats, dogs, donkeys, chickens, all in motion. The smell of human sweat and animal excrement is overwhelming. I have journeyed my whole life to get here. I used to be well heeled, well connected, a respected professional, who made decisions, a model indeed for every law-abiding citizen. But on the way, thugs attacked me and took my ID cards. Beyond my own country now, my currency no longer has any worth. I stand here exhausted, filthy, dried blood, green bruises, broken ribs stifling every breath. My voice: "Have *you* done this to me, torn my skin, struck me down, broken me into a mere shadow of my self? In fact, what kind of a self is it that I am now?" A gentle ripple passes through the heavy purple curtain: "I have hewn you with my own words; my judgment is a tender clemency upon you. I do not delight in your suffering. Respond to me, be still, receive the dawn, the morning dew." As I collapse, the scab falls away from my cheek, my breath stops hurting, and I sleep.

Ann Sirek

Fourth Sunday of Lent

Collect

O God, who through your Word
reconcile the human race to yourself in a wonderful way,
grant, we pray,
that with prompt devotion and eager faith
the Christian people may hasten
towards the solemn celebrations to come.
Through our Lord Jesus Christ, your Son,
who lives and reigns with you in the unity of the Holy Spirit,
one God, for ever and ever. Amen.

John 3:14-21

There is something noble about sharing the burden of someone who has been falsely accused. To stand in solidarity, to risk the loss of reputation, to become vulnerable to recrimination – all speak of autonomous virtue and the indomitable integrity of true human nature. But to assume the ignominy of the guilty and raise it up to God for forgiveness, healing, and transformation through divine exaltation – this is truly incomprehensible to even the most virtuous person. Yet, such an outpouring of unconditional love is exactly what Christ offers us in Word and Spirit. Sent into the world to bring not judgment but redemption. Who could remain unaffected by such a gift? Who could be indifferent to a benefaction that embraces us in our weakness and lifts us up in the most wonderful way to be reconciled in eternal life? Through Christ's ascent on the Cross, we are offered a fullness of love that first expands our hearts and then overflows into just action in the world, life-giving action that welcomes the light and bears witness to all without fear or conceit. Let us hasten towards the celebration to come!

Gordon Rixon, S.J.

Monday, March 19

Solemnity

Saint Joseph, Spouse of the Blessed Virgin Mary, Principal Patron of Canada

Collect

Grant, we pray, almighty God,
that by St. Joseph's intercession
your Church may constantly watch over
the unfolding of the mysteries of human salvation,
whose beginnings you entrusted to his faithful care.
Through our Lord Jesus Christ, your Son,
who lives and reigns with you in the unity of the Holy Spirit,
one God, for ever and ever. Amen.

Matthew 1:16, 18-21, 24

The Angel Gabriel came to Mary, and she is expecting a child. How is Joseph to know about this mystery? We can only imagine the pain of engaged love spurned.

The Angel visits once again, this time Joseph. He is to be husband. He is to be father to the Child conceived by the power of the Creating Spirit. How to comprehend this even greater mystery? Love is not spurned, but a greater love is invited. We can only imagine the emptying out of sacrifice – in love these beginnings are entrusted to Joseph's faithful care. God emptying out Self so the Word becomes flesh. Joseph emptying out self so the flesh may become Word.

The mystery of God's love enters our life, sometimes with pain, sometimes with emptying out, sometimes with joy, always with love. Like Joseph, we are called to respond with our life. God of compassionate love, may we cherish in Joseph a guide to trusting generosity so that this mystery of fostering love might unfold in me, in us, in Church.

Joseph Schner, S.J.

Tuesday in the Fourth Week of Lent

Collect

May the venerable exercises of holy devotion
shape the hearts of your faithful, O Lord,
to welcome worthily the Paschal Mystery
and proclaim the praises of your salvation.
Through our Lord Jesus Christ, your Son,
who lives and reigns with you in the unity of the Holy Spirit,
one God, for ever and ever. Amen.

John 5:1-16

"Do you want to be made well?" The obvious answer is "Yes." Right? Not the answer Jesus receives. After thirty-eight years of waiting for healing, the ill man responds first by blaming others for not helping him into the pool and then by blaming Jesus when those in authority question him about carrying his mat on the Sabbath after he is healed. The man does not take responsibility for his actions and remains fearful – after all, he knew his place in society when he was sick, but who is he now?

Each of us is spiritually blind or lame or paralyzed in some way. Jesus offers us "venerable exercises that shape our hearts": he asks us whether we are willing to be changed – willing to lose the comfort of familiar limitations, relearning who we are and possibly even coming into conflict with others – in order to rise and follow him, "proclaiming the praises of salvation." How exhilarating! How frightening!

What healing do I need? What's at stake? Am I willing to take the risk? The invitation is open to all. The choice to accept the offer. How I respond to the subsequent transformation is up to me.

Lecia Kiska

Wednesday in the Fourth Week of Lent

Collect

O God, who reward the merits of the just
and offer pardon to sinners who do penance,
have mercy, we pray, on those who call upon you,
that the admission of our guilt
may serve to obtain your pardon for our sins.
Through our Lord Jesus Christ, your Son,
who lives and reigns with you in the unity of the Holy Spirit,
one God, for ever and ever. Amen.

John 5:16-30

When Jesus came onto the scene in Galilee and Judea two thousand years ago, it would seem that very little had changed for the Jews from centuries earlier. They still lived under the authoritarian control of a foreign army. Physical sickness and hunger were rampant; further evidence, it might seem, that God had forgotten his people. But there in the midst of all that seemed wrong walked a man who healed the sick, made the lame to walk, and raised the dead. Where did he get the authority to perform these wonders? By what authority does he perform such acts on the Sabbath? "Very truly, I tell you, the Son can do nothing on his own, but only what he sees the Father doing; for whatever the Father does, the Son does likewise," Jesus responds. The Son has the authority from the Father both to give life and to judge justly.

As he did two thousand years ago, Jesus, the Son of God, walks into our lives today with the authority to offer to us everlasting life, "the merits of the just." Let us call upon Jesus with repentant hearts to receive the gift of life he offers to us.

Wayne Lott

Thursday in the Fourth Week of Lent

Collect

We invoke your mercy in humble prayer, O Lord,
that you may cause us, your servants,
corrected by penance and schooled by good works,
to persevere sincerely in your commands
and come safely to the paschal festivities.
Through our Lord Jesus Christ, your Son,
who lives and reigns with you in the unity of the Holy Spirit,
one God, for ever and ever. Amen.

John 5:18, 31-47

At times the journey of faith can feel like a solitary endeavour. It is true that once a week, and perhaps a day or two in between, we see our adopted families at church, but the majority of our time is spent away from our faith community. We work far from the place in which we pray, either physically or spiritually.

A "collect prayer" is meant to gather us as a people, to help us be truly "*we*". This time of the year, the most rigorous in the Church's calendar, presents us with the challenge to be a little more present among those who shape our spiritual being. Like Jesus attests to in the gospel reading, we cannot be our own witnesses; it is only through others that we can begin to define who we are as followers of Christ. Penance and good works, while they serve to benefit the individual soul, more importantly allow us the opportunity to restore the broken bonds that have separated us and our neighbour. Like our individual selves, our fractured communities are given the chance to be remade anew at this time. This process is not without pain, but the pain is necessary if we are truly to be present for the festivities that are swiftly approaching.

Ernest Holland

Friday in the Fourth Week of Lent

Collect

O God, who have prepared
fitting helps for us in our weakness,
grant, we pray, that we may receive
their healing effects with joy
and reflect them in a holy way of life.
Through our Lord Jesus Christ, your Son,
who lives and reigns with you in the unity of the Holy Spirit,
one God, for ever and ever. Amen.

John 7:1-2, 10, 25-30

God is always ready to provide helps for those who really want to be helped. That is, help that is not a quick fix or an answer whose outcome has been dictated already in the mind of the individual. Thus, we need to prepare ourselves to receive the helps that God offers in response to our petitions. We need to cultivate a disposition of openness to receive what God offers, even though God's help may not arrive in the manner we might have imagined (or even liked). Jesus' own relationship with the Father provides both the example and the way forward in our journeys through weakness to joyful union in a holy way of life. It is not a facile road, for the world is a complex place. As he moves towards his Passion, Jesus bears witness to the love of the Father that, in turn, enables him to endure pain and suffering. Let us seek to be open and to imbibe God's saving help in preparing to journey with Jesus to Calvary.

Erik Oland, S.J.

Saturday in the Fourth Week of Lent

Collect

> May the working of your mercy, O Lord, we pray,
> direct our hearts aright,
> for without your grace
> we cannot find favour in your sight.
> Through our Lord Jesus Christ, your Son,
> who lives and reigns with you in the unity of the Holy Spirit,
> one God, for ever and ever. Amen.

John 7:40-53

Surely the Messiah arose in Galilee – we know he did. Yet, pausing with this passage, we hear so much wondering and doubt, even denials. Supposing I did not know how Jesus' story unfolds and found myself transported to that time and place. Would I have been able to declare with certainty, "This is the Messiah"? Or at least is the prophet? Would I have been like Nicodemus, secretly believing and visiting Jesus? Or would I have been so convinced of the stereotype of the long-awaited Messiah that I could not open myself to recognize him when he arrived? It's hard to say what I would have done then. I can better consider how I might react today. In my workplace, at home, or in the company of strangers, how does my faith measure up? I have the benefit of knowledge of the truth. Yet do I believe? Do I speak up for Jesus? Or am I too narrow in my thinking to see Jesus in the here and now? Today I pray that the Lord will direct my heart and mind aright, so that I may see Jesus present in our midst and be a true witness.

Joan Gallagher-Main

Fifth Sunday of Lent

National Collection for Development and Peace

Collect

By your help, we beseech you, Lord our God,
may we walk eagerly in that same charity
with which, out of love for the world,
your Son handed himself over to death.
Through our Lord Jesus Christ, your Son,
who lives and reigns with you in the unity of the Holy Spirit,
one God, for ever and ever. Amen.

John 12:20-33

"May we walk eagerly in charity". That sounds simple enough, and perhaps what we good Christian people think we want in life. To walk in charity, and maybe even to do so eagerly, with some enthusiasm and zeal. Yet in this collect we do not pray to walk in just any sort of charity, any sort of love – and certainly not the many counterfeits for love peddled in our world. Rather, we ask for "that same charity with which, out of love for the world, your Son handed himself over to death." Are we so eager now? Eager for a love that may call us to hand ourselves over to death? Was Jesus himself so eager, after all? Even in John's gospel, as we read today, his soul is troubled. And yet, his desire, his "love for the world," is deep and constant: for the grain of wheat to die so that it may become far more than a single grain but bear much fruit. That is the eagerness we seek – not for suffering and death in themselves, but as expressions of that self-sacrificing love that alone will bear much fruit in the healing of a broken world.

Robin Koning, S.J.

Monday, March 26

Solemnity
The Annunciation of the Lord*

Collect

O God, who willed that your Word
should take on the reality of human flesh
in the womb of the Virgin Mary,
grant, we pray,
that we, who confess our Redeemer to be God and man,
may merit to become partakers even in his divine nature.
Who lives and reigns with you in the unity of the Holy Spirit,
one God, for ever and ever. Amen.

Luke 1:26-38

* *transferred from Sunday, March 25, in 2012.*

Today we consider the magnificent transformation of Mary's desire. We all have plans and dreams. At times, we feel God's call to leave the path we are on and to enter a new life. Certainly, Mary was like us in this way. A devout Jewish woman, no doubt she planned to marry Joseph, engage in community life, and hopefully raise a family. Suddenly, she hears the announcement that God has chosen her for an extraordinary role in the divine redemption of creation. She expresses her anxiety and confusion about this sudden change in her life. She questions and she listens. Then she surrenders, relinquishes control, and embraces God's will. She declares herself a servant of the Lord, a servant of the God whose love is meant for everyone. Looking beyond her earlier desires and expectations, she invites divine power to flow through her for the sake of others. In different ways, each of us is asked to say "yes" to God, to allow God's call to take on "the reality of human flesh" in us. Often this means overcoming fear and confusion and willingly surrendering our present plans. Only then can we humbly accept the new role we are being asked to assume in justly and lovingly transforming our world, helping it partake more and more in his divine nature.

Kathy Perry

Tuesday in the Fifth Week of Lent

Collect

Grant us, we pray, O Lord,
perseverance in obeying your will,
that in our days the people dedicated to your service
may grow in both merit and number.
Through our Lord Jesus Christ, your Son,
who lives and reigns with you in the unity of the Holy Spirit,
one God, for ever and ever. Amen.

John 8:21-30

"*Grant us, we pray, O Lord, perseverance in obeying your will.*" Today I thank God for his relentless pursuit of my soul's safety and salvation, for his *perseverance*; for not allowing me to wallow in self-pity, for not leaving me lost and imprisoned by my own intransigence and resistance. For his refusal to abdicate his post as my soul's guardian, whose grace discomforts and whose Spirit implores. I thank God for his eternal patience and his constant heart, for his faithfulness. He has never abandoned his watch by the wall of my soul, ever-present – to whisper or knock, to remind. It is I who turn away, averting my eyes; it is I who turn inward and become small, deaf, and blind to his gracious offering of forgiveness. I thank God who can watch this movement, so predictable, so childish in many ways, with compassionate eyes and not be deterred; today I thank God for being who God is.

Deacon Tony Pignataro

Wednesday in the Fifth Week of Lent

Collect

Enlighten, O God of compassion,
the hearts of your children, sanctified by penance,
and in your kindness
grant those you stir to a sense of devotion
a gracious hearing when they cry out to you.
Through our Lord Jesus Christ, your Son,
who lives and reigns with you in the unity of the Holy Spirit,
one God, for ever and ever. Amen.

John 8:31-42

The opening prayer asks God to help us better understand our Lenten observances. As a people, we do not practise austerity and do penance from some self-loathing stance. Moreover, we do not perform these difficult actions because we fear God and want to win God's love. We can never earn divine love; God generously pours out his love freely and bountifully. Fear and self-loathing only put us at a distance from God and cannot bring us into the enfolding mystery of the Father, Son, and Holy Spirit. We perform these Lenten practices because they help to shape and form us into the people we are meant to be. Our genuine identity is to be conformed to Jesus Christ – the one who eternally receives the Spirit of love from the Father and breathes that Spirit of Love to others. We cannot be Christ-like for a broken and hurt world if we are beholden to its ailments: consumerism, individualism, and relativism. We cannot testify to unconditional and eternal Love, even at the cost of our status and privilege, if we do not allow Christ to live within us, and we in Christ. Divine love seeks to use everyone, especially those with prepared hearts, for the greater glory of God.

Peter Nguyen, S.J.

Thursday in the Fifth Week of Lent

Collect

Be near, O Lord, to those who plead before you,
and look kindly on those who place their hope in your mercy,
that, cleansed from the stain of their sins,
they may persevere in holy living
and be made full heirs of your promise.
Through our Lord Jesus Christ, your Son,
who lives and reigns with you in the unity of the Holy Spirit,
one God, for ever and ever. Amen.

John 8:51-59

Abraham is a key figure in three major world faiths – Judaism, Islam, and Christianity – and in recent times he has been a stimulus for interfaith dialogue. Our Christian liturgy often speaks of Abraham as "our father in faith," and it is in this mode that we encounter him in the gospel. The Jewish leaders claimed to be heirs of Abraham, but they were not living in the faith of Abraham, that trusting dependence on God that was able to recognize and follow the leading of God, placing his hope in God's mercy. As Jesus says, they did not know God. Thus they could neither recognize nor accept the identity of Jesus. It is Jesus himself who both knows God and keeps the word of the Father. He is indeed himself – that Word made flesh. In the Incarnation, God's name – expressed as "I am" to the chosen people – becomes the human name of Jesus. Whoever allies themselves with this Word and places their hope in his saving mercy will "never taste death" but will have eternal life. In this way we become heirs of God's great promise. What an encouragement to persevere in our struggle to grow in holiness as heirs of that promise!

Gill Goulding, CJ

Friday in the Fifth Week of Lent

Collect

Pardon the offences of your peoples, we pray, O Lord,
and in your goodness set us free
from the bonds of the sins
we have committed in our weakness.
Through our Lord Jesus Christ, your Son,
who lives and reigns with you in the unity of the Holy Spirit,
one God, for ever and ever. Amen.

John 10:31-42

S*et us free from the bonds of sin...* Allowing their hatred to move from emotion to violent action, they threaten to stone Jesus. They are unable to see Jesus for who he is. They are caught up in their own blindness and refuse to examine their own hearts.

Jesus responds by offering them the gift of freedom. They are free to judge that his works are not of the Father. They are free to turn their backs on him and walk away. They are free to disbelieve him, at the same time believing what they see him do to be from the Father. Jesus' sole desire is that they live in the freedom of seeing things as they are; Jesus' relationship to the Father. "The Father is in me and I am in the Father." God is present and available.

Where can we see and express gratitude for the works of God today? Do we see the Father's gracious touch in our own lives and in the lives of those around us? Will this open our eyes to see Jesus in the Father and the Father in Jesus? Further, can we become aware of the call to be in him as he is in the Father?

Hugh Crosthwait

Saturday in the Fifth Week of Lent

Collect

O God, who have made all those reborn in Christ
a chosen race and a royal priesthood,
grant us, we pray, the grace to will
    and to do what you command,
that the people called to eternal life
may be one in the faith of their hearts
and the homage of their deeds.
Through our Lord Jesus Christ, your Son,
who lives and reigns with you in the unity of the Holy Spirit,
one God, for ever and ever. Amen.

John 11:45-57

Fear. We've all experienced it. Without this natural instinct, humanity would not have survived. Yet in today's gospel, this very survival instinct gets in the way. It acts as a blinder to the chief priests and the Pharisees when they are given news of the amazing signs performed by Jesus. You might think that those instructed in the Law would be the very ones to respond with awe and wonder, to be attuned to notice these long foretold signs. But they don't. Rather, the Sanhedrin was much more concerned about possible repercussions from Rome. Ironic, isn't it? Survival rather than religion occupies their concerns, and they cannot will and do as God desires for them.

Like the leaders, we, too, may fall victim to our fears. We, too, may allow our fears to dominate our lives and blind us to the signs of Christ's presence in our midst. As Lent draws to a close, let us take time to pay attention to the way we allow fear to operate in us. Do we listen to our fear, then consciously and prayerfully decide how best to respond, or do we allow ourselves to just react, blindly fuelling the instinctual fight or flight response? We are frail human beings called to ever greater freedom as a chosen race and a royal priesthood.

Mary Jo McDonald

Palm Sunday of the Lord's Passion

World Day of Youth

Collect

> Almighty ever-living God,
> who as an example of humility for the human race to follow
> caused our Saviour to take flesh and submit to the Cross,
> graciously grant that we may heed his lesson of patient
>   suffering
> and so merit a share in his Resurrection.
> Who lives and reigns with you in the unity of the Holy Spirit,
> one God, for ever and ever. Amen.

Mark 14:1–15:47

The words of the collect can appear, at first reading, extremely harsh. Indeed, the language of the prayer comes from an earlier time. And yet the collect can give us a helpful template for meditating on the mystery of Christ's Passion and death. Take the verb "to cause," for example. How did God "cause our Saviour to take flesh and submit to the Cross"? God's original decision to send the Son, taken by all three Divine Persons, is a decision to make divine love a part of human history in a new and unprecedented way. When that love enters into a world of sin and violence, it will be persecuted. Sin and violence have a profound hatred of the good, the true, and the beautiful in the world; they cannot let it be. Jesus, Son of God that he is, desires to remain faithful to the love that sent him, the love that dwells in his heart. And so, rather than resist violence with violence, he chooses the humility of suffering alongside all those who are victims of violence and sin. As we contemplate him on the way to Calvary, let us remember them.

Gilles Mongeau, S.J.

Monday of Holy Week

Collect

Grant, we pray, almighty God,
that, though in our weakness we fail,
we may be revived through the Passion
    of your Only Begotten Son.
Who lives and reigns with you in the unity of the Holy Spirit,
one God, for ever and ever. Amen.

John 12:1-11

In our weakness, may your Passion revive us…

A labourer in the ancient world would receive one denarius for a day's work. In today's gospel, we hear that a pound of nard is valued at one year's wages. We might well ask how Mary came to possess such riches. The gospel does not answer that question, but rather asks us a different one: what do we truly value? And it shows us how two of Jesus' contemporaries answered that question.

Mary knew that her house held the greatest treasure on earth, and it wasn't the nard. Knowing who Jesus was, Mary recognized the relative value of the perfume. For Mary, the riches of this world were not valuable in themselves, but were merely instruments that could be used for the glory of God.

Judas was correct, of course, to point out that one way in which we can glorify God with the goods of this world is to help those in need. But what he truly valued is clear. And Judas, who intends to betray the poor, intends to betray Jesus. Instead of the 300 denarii, Judas gets his 30 pieces of silver. He learns too late that they are of only relative value.

But when he sees their worthlessness in comparison to the treasure that is Christ, they bear fruit! Jesus had said that Mary's treasure was for his burial. Judas's treasure buys a plot of land to be used as a burial ground – a burial ground for poor foreigners.

Brett Salkeld

Tuesday of Holy Week

Collect

Almighty ever-living God,
grant us so to celebrate
the mysteries of the Lord's Passion
that we may merit to receive your pardon.
Through our Lord Jesus Christ, your Son,
who lives and reigns with you in the unity of the Holy Spirit,
one God, for ever and ever. Amen.

John 13:21-33, 36-38

Jesus knew. Jesus knew what was to come. Perhaps he didn't know the itinerary, or how exactly it would unfold, but Jesus *knew* it was time to give himself; he *knew* and trusted in God's love and faithfulness; and he *knew* the hearts of his followers – their weakness and their strength. We don't know what is to come, but we draw strength from celebrating the Passion of Christ, who is our model of trust, service, sacrifice, and love. Jesus lays down his life for us so that we will see a better way. It is not an easy way, that of sacrificing love, nor one that we will try without failing. Perhaps we know what we cannot do, but we may not be aware of what we can do in Christ. Still, we are drawn to ask, "Where are you going?" and promise to follow as best we can. Jesus knew his followers would fail at times, but he also knew he would help pick them back up to try again.

Kelly Bourke

Wednesday of Holy Week

Collect

O God, who willed your Son to submit for our sake
to the yoke of the Cross,
so that you might drive from us the power of the enemy,
grant us, your servants, to attain the grace of the Resurrection.
Through our Lord Jesus Christ, your Son,
who lives and reigns with you in the unity of the Holy Spirit,
one God, for ever and ever. Amen.

Matthew 26:14-26

Judas handed Jesus over to the authorities, but Christ chooses to submit to the Cross, "so that he might drive from us the power of the enemy." What does it mean to betray Christ? It can mean many things, but primarily it is a refusal to love as he did. We remain true to the Lord if we follow the commandments to love the Lord with all our heart, all our soul, all our mind, and all our strength, and to love our neighbour as ourselves. Christ's sacrifice was the ultimate love, conquering sin and death by death – the primary instrument of the enemy's power – and giving us the grace of resurrection in him, even when we fail to love. How can we possibly turn away from this tremendous gift of love?

Erin MacCarthy

Easter Triduum

Mass of the Lord's Supper

> O God, who have called us to participate
> in this most sacred Supper,
> in which your Only Begotten Son,
> when about to hand himself over to death,
> entrusted to the Church a sacrifice new for all eternity,
> the banquet of his love,
> grant, we pray,
> that we may draw from so great a mystery
> the fullness of charity and of life.
> Through our Lord Jesus Christ, your Son,
> who lives and reigns with you in the unity of the Holy Spirit,
> one God, for ever and ever. Amen.

John 13:1-15

Jesus knows he is going to be executed. He has come to Jerusalem to confront the violent powers of the world that oppose God, and has proclaimed his authority to reconcile and to heal by the cleansing of the Temple. He gathers his closest followers and shares a Last Supper with them. In that Last Supper, he shows, in his actions with the bread and wine, the meaning he wants to give to his death: he wants to make of it a total offering of himself out of love for God and for us. This is the true meaning of "sacrifice." Jesus remains faithful to the love received from his Father. He has come to serve, as he shows in the washing of the feet, and the climax of that service is his giving of himself out of love. Truly, this is his banquet of love.

Celebration of the Lord's Passion

> O God, who by the Passion of Christ your Son, our Lord,
> abolished the death inherited from ancient sin
> by every succeeding generation,
> grant that just as, being conformed to him,
> we have borne by the law of nature
> the image of the man of earth,
> so by the sanctification of grace
> we may bear the image of the Man of heaven.
> Through our Lord Jesus Christ, your Son,
> who lives and reigns with you in the unity of the Holy Spirit,
> one God, for ever and ever. Amen.

John 18:1–19:42

What does it mean to be conformed to the image of the Man of heaven instead of the image of the man of earth? In the gospel of John, we see both kinds of people contrasted. Jesus, the Man of heaven, is secure in his identity as God's Beloved. He does not need to affirm who he is at the expense of others. Judas, the religious authorities, and Pilate all seek to make their own position in society secure by demeaning Jesus, by making him less than human. The violence unleashed against Jesus expresses the pattern by which evil in "every succeeding generation" reaches into our insecurities and exploits them for its own death-dealing purposes. Perfectly decent people in the assembled crowd cry out for Jesus' execution. Even Peter gives in to fear, abandoning Jesus. Only a grace-filled love keeps John and Mary at Jesus' side. Two images: the man of earth, caught up in violence and death; the Man of heaven, offering himself out of love for God and for us.

Easter Vigil

> O God, who make this most sacred night radiant
> with the glory of the Lord's Resurrection,
> stir up in your Church a spirit of adoption,
> so that, renewed in body and mind,
> we may render you undivided service.
> Through our Lord Jesus Christ, your Son,
> who lives and reigns with you in the unity of the Holy Spirit,
> one God, for ever and ever. Amen.

Mark 16:1-8

It is like this in so many cultures, in so many events of world history: it is women, moved by love and compassion, who discover in that love and compassion the courage to confront the death-dealing powers of the world and "render undivided service." Think of the Mothers of the Disappeared in Argentina, standing up to military dictatorship; think of the grandmothers of sub-Saharan Africa, raising their AIDS-orphaned grandchildren and creating a worldwide network of grandmother-activists against AIDS. But here, the women receive a surprise: Jesus is alive and the night is radiant with the glory of his Resurrection. God has received Jesus' offering of love and overturns the sentence pronounced by the power of sin and death against him. That gift of new life, of being renewed in body and mind beyond death, spills over to us as Jesus' brothers and sisters. The "spirit of adoption" that we pray for disposes us to accept this gift and share it with all people.

Gilles Mongeau, S.J.

Easter Sunday

> O God, who on this day,
> through your Only Begotten Son,
> have conquered death
> and unlocked for us the path to eternity,
> grant, we pray, that we who keep
> the solemnity of the Lord's Resurrection
> may, through the renewal brought by your Spirit,
> rise up in the light of life.
> Through our Lord Jesus Christ, your Son,
> who lives and reigns with you in the unity of the Holy Spirit,
> one God, for ever and ever. Amen.

John 20:1-18

Love knows. Mary Magdalene and the disciple Jesus loved know the meaning of the empty tomb; they do not need explanations. God has conquered sin and death, we are reconciled with God, and the way to communion with God forever is opened to us once again. The Spirit, poured out on all as promised through the prophet Joel, renews us and brings us into Jesus' loving presence. So now, when we gather for the Lord's Supper, we aren't just looking backwards at the Cross, we are looking forward with thanksgiving to the time when we will all "rise up in the light of life." When we "keep the solemnity," we enter again into the garden with Mary; we meet him in the breaking of the bread, and we know.

Gilles Mongeau, S.J.

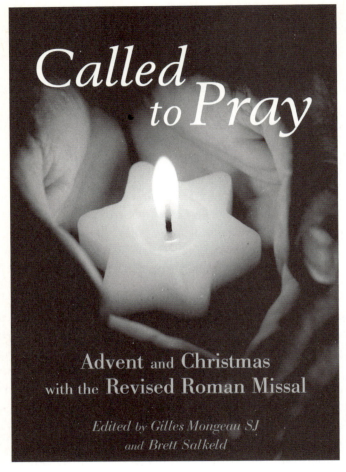

ISBN: 978-2-89646-434-0
$12.95*

Available from your local bookseller or from Novalis:
www.novalis.ca

* Price is subject to change without notice.